Fantasy Chronicles

Wizards and Witches

Ann Kerns

Lerner Publications Company · Minneapolis

Lerner Publications Company
A division of Lerner Publishing Group, Inc.
241 First Avenue North
Minneapolis, MN 55401 U.S.A.

Website address: www.lernerbooks.com

Library of Congress Cataloging-in-Publication Data

Kerns, Ann, 1959–
 Wizards and witches / by Ann Kerns.
  p. cm. — (Fantasy chronicles)
 Includes bibliographical references and index.
 ISBN-13: 978–0–8225–9983–8 (lib. bdg. : alk. paper)
 1. Witches—Juvenile literature. 2. Wizards—Juvenile literature. I. Title.
BF1566.K463 2010
133.4'309—dc22   2008050757

Manufactured in the United States of America
3 – DP – 9/1/10

TABLE OF CONTENTS

CHAPTER 1

MAGICAL PEOPLE

A dark figure in a long black gown weaves through the night, casting shadows in the moonlight with her broomstick and crooked nose. At a creaky gate, she turns. She creeps up to a haunted-looking house and reaches a long, crooked fingernail toward the bell.

"Trick or treat!" she cries, holding up her sack for candy. Such images of witches are everywhere—in cartoons, on TV commercials, and of course at Halloween. Most people also know the image of a wizard as an old man with long robes and a tall pointed hat.

Witches and wizards have been part of literature and popular entertainment for a very long time. In some stories, they are old and mean, trying to harm people or cause trouble. In other stories, they are funny or good. But there was a time when witches and wizards were real people who believed they had special powers. And other people believed them too. Some people still believe in the power of witchcraft.

That Old Magic

In folklore and literature, witches and wizards are humans who can perform magic. This isn't the kind of magic where someone pulls a rabbit out of a hat. In witchcraft and wizardry, magic is the ability to control things through special powers.

Magical powers can cause things to happen or prevent things from happening. They can influence the physical world (such as the weather) or change another person's behavior.

Of course, humans in general can control the world around us to some degree. Humans invented cars and airplanes to travel faster. We have medicines that cure diseases. We have telephones and computers.

Much of what we do in modern times would seem like magic to someone from long ago. But we know that each invention has an explanation. We know that scientists and inventors rely on the laws of math and science and their own imaginations.

In witchcraft and wizardry, another system of laws exists behind physical reality. That system is the supernatural or paranormal world. These are things some people believe in that science or common sense cannot explain. Spirits, ghosts, and the ability to read minds are examples of supernatural or paranormal events.

Magical people believe that supernatural power or energy exists throughout the universe. A witch or wizard must learn to tap into and control that energy. That's what gives them their magical powers.

From Wishes To Magic

Belief in magical people exists in cultures throughout history and around the world. Some historians think that the ancient belief in magic grew out of simple human behavior. For example, prehistoric cave dwellers might have wished very hard for a terrible thunderstorm to stop. When the storm ended, the cave dwellers might have thought that their wishes stopped it.

Wishes gave these early people a sense of control over frightening situations.

Over time, wishes turned into rituals and spells. Simple behaviors turned into larger, more complicated systems of beliefs. Soon, special people became the keepers of those beliefs. They became the community's magicians.

A village relied on its magic maker to cure diseases, help couples have babies, and help the crops grow. The magicians also became storytellers. They passed down the community's history, legends, and traditional wisdom.

These magicians were important and respected in the community. But because they were so powerful, they were also sometimes feared. If a magician was strong enough to do so much good, couldn't he or she also cause bad things to happen? If the crops failed or villagers got sick, was it the magician's fault? Their power sometimes put magic makers in a difficult position.

Wizards often appear with books of magic. Like scientists, wizards had to study their art.

All Around the World

Asian folklore and myths are full of demons, spirits, magic spells, and fortune-telling. In many Asian cultures, communities still rely on specially trained people to keep away evil spirits and draw in good spirits.

India, Tibet, and parts of Southeast Asia have people called shamans. Shamans are healers. They use traditional medicines and rituals to cure illnesses. They are also the community's link to the spirit world. In many Asian cultures, families believe that the spirits of their dead ancestors guide and protect them. It is the shaman's duty to keep that link to the spirit world open. This practice is called mysticism.

A Mongolian shaman sprinkles milk during a ceremony. The milk is an offering to earth spirits.

Shamanism, mysticism, and magic are also strong in African traditions. Some villagers perform the role of helping families contact their dead ancestors. They also work to bring good luck to the community. Other shamans are masters of traditional healing methods.

In the Americas, ceremonial people perform many sacred rituals. Most Native American beliefs feature a strong connection to nature and to the spirit world. Native American ceremonial people pass down traditional wisdom and practices to the next generation.

Mysticism and witchcraft continue to appeal to some people. They use herbs and special potions for healing rituals. They hold ceremonies to connect to the natural and spirit worlds. Some of these

A South African shaman uses bones to answer questions.

people belong to a religion called Wicca. Others call their practices witchcraft or alternative spirituality.

Wiccans and others may use some of the rituals from around the world. But many of these practitioners live in the United States and Europe. And much of what they believe comes from the long traditions of witchcraft and magic in the West.

CHAPTER 2

Witches in the West

While ancient Asians, Africans, and others

were performing their mystical ceremonies,

witchcraft was alive and well in ancient Europe.

Like shamans and other ceremonial people,

European witches were known for their healing abilities. In many stories, these women—and sometimes men—also used supernatural powers to see into the future. But over the course of history, European witches developed a very bad reputation.

In the Ancient World

In ancient times, Greece and Rome were the most powerful civilizations in Europe. Both the Greeks and the Romans had many deities (gods and goddesses). And like other ancient cultures, they believed that certain people held supernatural powers. Some of the most powerful people, it was believed, were experts at prophecy (seeing the future).

The Greeks and Romans also believed in witchcraft and magic. People flocked to witches to buy love potions. They asked witches to curse unfriendly neighbors or business rivals.

Legendary Witches

Some famous witches appear in Greek and Roman myth and literature. Medea plays a role in the legend of Jason and the Argonauts.
Jason is a Greek hero who searches for a magical sheepskin—the
Golden Fleece. Medea is the beautiful daughter of the king of
Colchis. She is an enchantress—a woman with the power to cast
magic spells. Medea uses her witchcraft
to help Jason get the fleece.

Medea's aunt, Circe, is also a witch.
Like Medea, she is young and beautiful. She appears in the Greek tale *The*

Medea makes a
potion for Jason in
this 1907 painting
by English artist
John William
Waterhouse.

Odyssey. In the story, sailors led by the warrior Odysseus are caught in a hurricane. Their ship lands on an island owned by Circe. Circe first uses a magical potion to turn Odysseus's men into swine (pigs). But she then falls in love with Odysseus and frees his men.

Bad Magic

The ancient Romans were very superstitious. They believed in many things they could not logically explain. One old Roman superstition said that you could cure a head cold by kissing a donkey on the nose. Romans also believed that certain people could do others harm just by looking at them. That superstition was known as the "evil eye."

Harmful magic such as the evil eye was called *malefice.* People believed witches could protect them against malefice by giving them

In ancient Greece, witchcraft had its own goddess— Hecate *(below).* She lived in the underworld, the realm of the dead in Greek mythology. In Greek art, Hecate is often depicted as a triple goddess—one goddess having three bodies.

This ancient copper amulet found in northern Europe contains a snakeskin.

amulets. Amulets are ornaments or pieces of magical material, such as snakeskin. A person wore an amulet to defeat bad magic.

But ancient Romans also believed that witches created malefice. As early as the 400s B.C., Roman officials made it illegal to use evil spells to harm someone. People were nervous about witches misusing their powers. Over the years, suspicion and fear of witchcraft grew. Stories began to depict witches as old, ugly, scary women.

For example, the Roman poet Lucan (A.D. 39-65) tells a story about the witch Erictho. Erictho lives alone in a graveyard outside the city of Rome. She lives by sucking the blood of humans—living and newly dead. She does not obey the gods and only performs her malefice to benefit herself. Figures such as Erictho set the stage for how witches would be characterized in the centuries that followed.

The power of many magical practices lies in the spoken word. Enchantment, the power to influence someone through magic, comes from the word *chant*. To chant is to recite words in a rhythmic pattern. Spells and charms must also be spoken. *Spell* comes from an old word meaning "talk." *Charm* comes from an old word meaning "song."

Into the Middle Ages

In the first centuries A.D., great changes took place in Europe. The Roman Empire began to lose its power. A new religion called Christianity grew. After the Roman Empire collapsed in about 500, Christianity spread through Europe. This began the historical era known as the Middle Ages.

Christianity has only one god. Christian beliefs are based on the Bible. The Bible is a combination of Jewish beliefs and the teachings of Jesus Christ. In these ways, Christianity was very different from ancient European religions. Those religions had many deities and were often based on local traditions and witchcraft.

The early church and many governments outlawed witchcraft. They thought it went against Christian beliefs. But early

Christians kept practicing the old ways. They went to church on Sunday. But they also went to the local witch for herbal medicines, good luck charms, and amulets. In fact, most European villages had "cunning folk"—people who had special talents with fortune-telling, potions, and spells.

Satan and Witchcraft

As Christianity grew, Christian leaders viewed witchcraft as a more serious problem. They came to believe that witchcraft was the work of Satan. In Christian thought, Satan is the ultimate symbol of evil.

Early Christians believed that Satan and his demons were drawn to humans. The demons, so legends say, wanted to spread evil on earth by preying on human

In this woodcut, witches dine with Satan *(left)* and his demons.

weaknesses. The demons wanted witches and other magic makers to help them.

Some church leaders did not believe that all cunning folk were bad people. But church leaders believed that demons were behind witchcraft and used it to lead humans astray. So they wanted to stop all magical practices. They did not want harmless superstitions to open the door to more powerful evil forces.

Wild Tales of Witches

Church leaders began to claim that witchcraft amounted to devil worship. Witches, they said, attended meetings called sabbats. Sabbats were held in secret, deep in the woods outside villages. The witches flew to the sabbats on besoms (brooms made of twigs). Once there, the witches danced around a fire, shrieking wildly and calling for Satan to appear.

Rumors also spread that witches could change themselves into animals. They also kept familiars—animals that helped the witches create magic. Their familiars included black cats, snakes, crows, and ravens.

Witch Hunts

In 1536, the Spanish Inquisition (a group within the Catholic Church) put out an order. The order said that all people should report anyone caught practicing witchcraft. Some people were happy to do so—especially if it meant reporting on a neighbor they did not like.

Villagers began to turn on each other. If a child suddenly got sick, the parents might accuse an unfriendly neighbor of using the evil eye to cause the illness. If a cow stopped giving milk, the farmer might accuse an elderly villager of casting a spell. Witch hunting became a hysteria.

Many women, especially the old or the lonely, lived in terror of being accused. If brought before the Inquisition, an accused witch was asked to confess. If she said she was innocent, she could be tortured. Many people confessed to witchcraft just to stop the torture. Other accused witches were put to death in horrible ways, such as being burned alive.

Salem

This obsession with witchcraft followed European settlers to the American colonies. The Massachusetts Bay Colony was established in the 1620s and 1630s by English Christians called Puritans.

Puritan ministers did not want any magical practices in the colony. Charms and spells were forbidden. Leaders preached that Satan wanted to destroy the peaceful and God-fearing settlement, and he would use witches to do it.

In 1692 Puritan fears about witchcraft reached a boiling point in Salem Village, Massachusetts. Salem's witch crisis began when a group of young girls began acting very strangely. They cried out in pain, fainted, and sometimes couldn't speak.

The girls claimed that some local women were witches and were

causing the pain and suffering. The girls soon began accusing many other men and women from the area of witchcraft.

A man pleads his innocence during the witch trials in Salem, Massachusetts, in this 1855 painting.

By May 1692, almost 150 people were in jail awaiting trial. Nineteen villagers were hanged as witches. One man was crushed by heavy stones to force him to confess. Another seven died in jail before the Salem hysteria ended.

In Europe, too, authorities began to put an end to witch hunts. But many people still feared witches. A lonely old woman with a black cat for a pet could still find herself the target of her neighbors' suspicions.

CHAPTER 3

WIZARDS IN THE WEST

Like witches, wizards were not supposed to go against religious teachings. They were not to "open the door" to demons and evil spirits.

But throughout history, wizards have fared better than witches. They have often been treated with suspicion and fear. But there have never been any real wizard-hunting panics.

One reason might be that witches were often women and wizards were usually men. In many cases, the men were educated and respected members of the community. The women had less power.

Also, in most stories about wizards, they secretly study magic on their own. They do not sell love spells, curses, and herbal potions. So authorities were less likely to worry about wizards leading simple folk astray. But there are other larger differences between witches and wizards. Many of those can be traced back to the history and purpose of wizardry.

In the Ancient World

Stories about wizards (often called sorcerers or magicians) appear in ancient Greek, Roman, Jewish, and early Christian texts. In the ancient world, many people believed that a wizard's secret knowledge began with a man named Ham, son of Noah, who appears in the Bible. According to ancient lore, Ham was the first person to learn about the science of magic. It was believed that the ancient peoples in the Middle East and Egypt were all descended from Ham. His secret knowledge of magic was passed down through the ages.

Stories about magic makers appear in many Middle Eastern and Mediterranean traditions. In the Bible, King Solomon was a very wise leader. But according to Hebrew, Greek, and Arabic traditions, he was also a wizard. He could make demons do his bidding. He understood the secret laws of nature. He knew many magic rituals and wore a great ring carved with magical symbols.

Ancient Egyptian myth also includes a god of wisdom and magic, Thoth. According to legend, Thoth invented writing and guided the souls of the

In this illustration from 1473, King Solomon summons a demon and makes it dance for him.

dead to the afterworld. The Greeks were fascinated by Thoth and other Egyptian ideas about magic and religion. They combined elements of Thoth with one of their own gods, Hermes. They recorded their ideas in writings called the *Hermetica*, which contained instructions for spells, rituals, and other magical arts.

The Magic Universe

The ancient Romans inherited the secret lore contained in the *Hermetica*. From Rome, the knowledge passed to medieval European scholars. They used this lore to develop their own ideas about magic.

Hermes *(above)* was the Greek god of communication, writing, and secret knowledge.

Like King Solomon, medieval wizards read and studied many subjects until they mastered them. They believed that there was a secret body of knowledge about the natural and supernatural worlds. They used magical tools and objects, such as rings and wands. They dressed in special robes decorated with symbols. And they performed rituals that helped them focus their magic powers. Modern people tend to separate

religion, magic, and science. But in earlier times, many people thought of them as all part of one big system. An important part of a wizard's training was learning about mathematics, how the planets move, the properties of metals and stones, and what patterns exist in nature.

The Persian astrologer Albumasar wrote books that were used by wizards in the Middle Ages.

Dangerous Power

Medieval wizards believed they were performing *theurgia*—divine work. They were combining theology (the study of God) with science. But wizardry was still full of dangers. Like other people of their day, medieval wizards believed that the universe was home to many demons and spirits. The power of a wizard's magic depended on his ability to call forth these creatures. But once the spirits or demons arrived, the wizard had to know how to control them—or he would find himself in deep trouble.

John Dee

John Dee (1527-1608) was a famous magician at a time when people believed in both science and magic. Dee combined his magical practices with the study of mathematics, geography, and astronomy.

Dee is most famous for his conversations with angels. According to Dee, humans could contact angels by gazing into a crystal or glass ball. This practice is called scrying. Dee wrote down all his angelic conversations, including some in a mysterious language he called Enochian.

In some stories, a demon or spirit called forth by a wizard does great damage. A wizard might find his room engulfed in flames or flooded by a fountain of water. The wizard might even find his soul in danger. Medieval stories warn of wizards becoming enchanted by their own power. Pleased with smaller successes, they try more dangerous magic and end up out of control.

Alchemy is the ancient belief that base (inferior) metals such as tin can be turned into gold. The ancient process for making gold was a mixture of science and magic. In the Middle Ages, people thought that gold was the only absolutely pure and perfect metal. It could not only bring a person great wealth—it could also bring health and wisdom. For that reason, many sorcerers and magicians studied alchemy.

One famous story tells of such a wizard, Faust. Faust became the subject of a fantastic legend in Germany in the 1500s. In the story, Faust is a magician, astrologer, and necromancer (someone who contacts the spirits of the dead). Faust strikes a bargain with Satan through the devil Mephistopheles. If Mephistopheles will give him more magical powers, Faust will sell his soul to Satan.

At the end of twenty-four years, Mephistopheles comes to collect Faust's soul. Mephistopheles begins dragging Faust down into hell. But the magician is truly sorry for his vanity and love of power. He asks God for forgiveness and is saved from Satan.

King Solomon, John Dee, and Faust were well-known figures. The legends that surround them show that people were fascinated by magic, wizardry, and witchcraft. In fact, magical people have appeared in some of our most famous books and plays.

Mephistopheles appears to Faust in this 1925 painting by Irish artist Harry Clarke.

CHAPTER 4

Witches and Wizards Hit The Books

Fantasy literature is a modern term for a specific kind of story. Fantasy literature includes magic, paranormal events, and strange creatures. But once upon a time, people believed that magic swirled all around them. Most literature had elements of fantasy. And witches and wizards were popular characters.

Merlin

One of the most famous literary characters in history happens to be a wizard. Merlin appears in many stories from the Middle Ages as the advisor of King Arthur. King Arthur is a legendary king of England. In these tales, Merlin is a master of magical spells and can see the future. Through magic, Merlin helps young Arthur gain the throne of England.

In some Arthurian tales, Merlin's story ends when he is caught in a magical trick. Merlin falls in love with a young and beautiful witch. She convinces Merlin to tell her all his magical secrets. Being able to see the future, Merlin knows that she will trick him. But he cannot change the course of

The character of Merlin might be based on stories about Celtic Druids. Druids were priests who practiced an ancient religion in the Celtic countries of Ireland, Scotland, and Wales.

Toil and Trouble

Shakespeare's 1603 play *Macbeth* opens with three witches gathered in a lonely place during a thunderstorm. The witches are looking for the Scottish soldier Macbeth, and they soon find him.

The women are so strange looking that Macbeth is not sure they are human. He is shocked when they call him by name and tell him that he will become king of Scotland. Their announcement plants an idea in Macbeth's head, and he is soon plotting murder to get to the throne.

Swiss artist Johann Heinrich Fuessli painted this picture of the witches from *Macbeth* in 1783.

Shakespeare's magical people draw on long traditions of European folklore. In the early 1800s, two German brothers began collecting these folktales about witches and other fierce creatures. Jakob Grimm (1785–1863) and Wilhelm Grimm (1786–1859) were fascinated by old tales that were passed from generation to generation. In the early 1800s, the Brothers Grimm published several volumes of these stories. The stories were meant to delight and send a shiver of fear through young readers.

Grimm Witches

In *Rapunzel*, the Brothers Grimm unfold the tale of an evil old witch who locks a young girl in a lonely tower. Rapunzel has beautiful hair, which she braids every day. The braid grows so long that it hangs out the tower window. One morning a prince sees Rapunzel and climbs up her braid to the tower. They fall

The witch climbs up Rapunzel's braid in a 1919 illustration by English artist Arthur Rackham.

in love and make plans to run away. But the witch finds out, cuts off Rapunzel's braid, and sends the girl away.

The prince returns and sees the braid hanging, as usual, from the tower. He climbs up the braid. But instead of finding his pretty girlfriend, he finds the angry witch. Rapunzel and the prince are reunited, but only after the witch takes her revenge.

In another Grimm tale, Hansel and his sister Gretel become lost in the woods. After wandering about, they come upon a house made of candy. An old woman opens the door and invites the children in for a feast. But the old woman is a witch, and Hansel and Gretel *are* the feast! But when the witch fires up her oven, Gretel tricks her into crawling into the oven, and the children escape.

In many of these tales, witches are jealous of young, pretty women. And they think nothing of harming children. Scholars think many of these

The witch emerges from her house, surprising Hansel and Gretel. In some versions of the story, her house is made of gingerbread or cookies.

folktales were meant as warnings to young readers. If you don't behave and stay where you belong, the stories caution, wicked witches will get you.

Over time, the figure of the witch became less frightening and more amusing. In the late 1800s and early 1900s, witches began appearing in popular illustrations and magazine ads. The witch often had old black clothes, a pointy hat, and shoes with curly toes. She usually had crooked teeth and at least one hairy wart. She was weird and ugly but mostly harmless. But it wouldn't be long before popular culture expanded its ideas about witches.

This witch isn't frightening at all. She appears on a greeting card from 1910.

CHAPTER 5

HARRY POTTER AND COMPANY

In the 1900s and into the 2000s, ideas about witches and wizards took new directions.

Witches weren't always warty old women who chased after stray children. And wizards weren't always odd men who mumbled to themselves over their dusty books. Witches and wizards expanded into a whole array of characters—some bad and some good.

And Your Little Dog Too!

In 1900, U.S. writer L. Frank Baum published the children's fantasy book *The Wonderful Wizard of Oz*. The book contains good witches, bad witches, and a great and powerful wizard. The story begins on a Kansas farm where a young girl, Dorothy, lives with her aunt and uncle. One day, a tornado strikes the farm. Dorothy and her little black dog, Toto, are swept up by the storm. They land in the magical country of Oz. Oz is ruled by a wizard who lives in the mysterious City of Emeralds.

Hollywood's famous film version of *The Wizard of Oz* came out in 1939. Songs and dance routines were added. And the story's witches and wizard

In a scene from *The Wizard of Oz,* the Wicked Witch of the West threatens Dorothy. But the Good Witch of the North protects her.

were given star treatment. The Good Witch of the North (played by Billie Burke) wears a beautiful gown and waves a glittering magic wand. Margaret Hamilton as the Wicked Witch of the West has green skin and an evil cackle. And this wicked witch actually did ride a broomstick, by way of some early movie special effects.

At the Emerald City, Dorothy and her friends find the Wizard of Oz. The wizard is surrounded by eerie green light and clouds of smoke. He is an awesome and frightening character—until Toto slips behind a curtain and reveals the wizard's secret. The Wizard of Oz, as it turns out, isn't really scary at all. Like other wizards, he considers himself a man of science.

Serious Witches and Wizards

The novels of the British author J. R. R. Tolkien (1892–1973) represent another side of fantasy literature. His three Lord of the Rings novels were published in 1954 and 1955. They feature two wizards, Gandalf and Saruman, and a huge cast of supernatural creatures.

The novels are serious, complicated, and often very dark in tone. The stories are set in a world that exists parallel to the human world. But the parallel world is unknown to most humans. This type of writing is known as high fantasy.

Tolkien's friend, C. S. Lewis (1898–1963), also created parallel worlds in his children's high fantasy novels. Lewis published the Chronicles of Narnia in the 1950s. The seven-book series includes *The Magician's Nephew* and *The Lion, the Witch, and the Wardrobe.*

Gandalf the wizard fights with sword as well as magic in the 2003 film, *Lord of the Rings: The Return of the King.*

In both books, the villain is Jadis, the White Witch. She cruelly rules the alternate world that the books' children discover by accident.

Making Nice Magic

In the late 1950s and 1960s, magical people became popular on television and in the movies. Witches and wizards always made good fictional villains. But what if they were just regular people trying to fit into the non-magical world? The movie *Bell, Book, and Candle* (1958) stars Kim Novak as Gillian, a young witch in New York City. She falls in love with her non-magical neighbor, Shep (James Stewart). Gillian tries to help Shep understand magic—and tries to get him to relax around her witchy family and friends.

Bewitched took up a similar theme. This U.S. television series ran from 1964 to 1972. Elizabeth Montgomery plays a witch named Samantha, who is married to a non-magical business executive.

Elsa Lanchester *(left)* and Jack Lemmon *(right)* watch as Kim Novak tries out a spell in *Bell, Book, and Candle.*

Samantha spends most of the series balancing her two lives. She works hard as a homemaker and mother. But she also has to keep the peace between her husband and her mother, the witch Endora.

Bedknobs and Broomsticks mixes animation and live-action special effects. This 1971 movie is set in England during World War II (1939-1945). Eglantine Price (played by Angela Lansbury) is just beginning to study witch-craft. Then three young children come to live with Miss Price to escape the dangers of the war. Together, they are drawn into an adventure involving flying beds, a witchcraft college in London, and objects that spring to life.

In *Bewitched,* Elizabeth Montgomery played a witch who makes magic by wiggling her nose.

Along with these positive por-trayals, there was always room for stories about villainous witches. In the children's novel *The Witches* (1983), Roald Dahl reveals a worldwide network of evil magic makers. These witches seem like normal women leading ordinary lives. But that is only a disguise. In reality, the witches have claws for hands, bald heads, blue saliva, and toeless feet. They are out to kill all the children on earth. A young boy and his grandmother must stop the witches' plot.

Hogwarts

A school of witchcraft in England is the setting for a series of fantasy books by British writer J. K. Rowling. *Harry Potter and the Philosopher's Stone* was first published in Great Britain in 1997. It was published the next year in the United States as *Harry Potter and the Sorcerer's Stone.* The novel became a world-wide phenomenon, read by children and adults alike. Rowling wrote six more Harry Potter novels, several of which have been made into movies.

In the first novel, Harry Potter is a ten-year-old orphan living with his relatives, the Dursleys. The Dursleys are cruel to Harry, and he does not understand why they hate him. But then Harry begins to notice that he has some unusual powers. After his eleventh birthday, he receives a surprising letter—an invitation to study at the Hogwarts School of Witchcraft and Wizardry.

In the Harry Potter books, some non-magical people are known as Muggles. Many muggles are completely unaware that the world of witchcraft and wizards even exists. They cannot, for example, see Hogwarts School. When Muggles come upon Hogwarts, all they see are the ruins of an old castle.

The invitation opens up a whole new magical world to Harry. Over the course of the series, Harry goes from being an unloved outsider to a leader at Hogwarts. He learns how to control and wisely use his magical powers. And he learns to balance his magical life with his everyday life.

The movie version of *Harry Potter and the Half-Blood Prince* will be released in 2009. A movie version of the last novel, *Harry Potter and the Deathly Hallows* is planned for 2010. The success of the Harry Potter series and the fans' dedication suggests that interest in witchcraft and wizardry is far from over.

Harry Potter fans dressed up for a special train taking them to a book release party for *Harry Potter and the Deathly Hallows* in 2007.

Selected Bibliography

Ankarloo, Bengt, and Stuart Clark, eds. *Witchcraft and Magic in Europe.* Philadelphia: University of Pennsylvania Press, 2002.

Davies, Owen. *Witchcraft, Magic and Culture 1736–1951.* Manchester, UK: Manchester University Press, 1999.

Dickerson, Matthew, and David O'Hara. *From Homer to Harry Potter: A Handbook on Myth and Fantasy.* Grand Rapids, MI: Brazos Press, 2006.

Lehane, Brendan, and the Editors of Time-Life Books. *Wizards and Witches. Alexandria, VA: Time-Life Books, 1984.*

Maxwell-Stuart, P.G. *Witchcraft: A History.* Stroud, UK: Tempus Publishing, 2000.

———. *Wizards: A History.* Stroud, UK: Tempus Publishing, 2002.

Further Reading

Duane, Diane. *So You Want to Be a Wizard.* 1983. Reprint, San Diego: Magic Carpet Books, 1996. Nita Callaghan and her friend Kit are just ordinary New Yorkers—who happen to be studying wizardry. After a run-in with a school bully, the pair finds themselves lost in a supernatural version of Manhattan.

Rowling, J. K. *Harry Potter and the Sorcerer's Stone.* New York: Scholastic, 1998. Readers are introduced to Harry Potter as he discovers he has some mysterious powers. He enrolls at the Hogwarts School of Witchcraft and Wizardry, and a whole new magical world opens up to him. In this book and in the rest of the series, readers follow Harry and his friends on their journey to become trained wizards.

Sage, Angie. *Magyk.* New York: HarperCollins, 2005. The first book in Sage's Septimus Heap series features wizards and a wide cast of other magical creatures

Sexton, Colleen. *J. K. Rowling.* Minneapolis: Twenty-First Century Books, 2005. Read all about Harry Potter's creator in this detailed biography.

Stefoff, Rebecca. *Witches and Witchcraft.* New York: Benchmark, 2007. Stefoff uses folklore, mythology, and psychology to examine the topic of witchcraft.

Tolkien, J. R. R. *The Fellowship of the Ring.* 1954. Reprint, New York: Houghton Mifflin, 2004. This is the first book in Lord of the Rings trilogy, Tolkien's fantasy epic. Readers are introduced to two powerful wizards, Gandalf and Saruman, and a host of other supernatural creatures.

Movies

Bedknobs and Broomsticks. Burbank, CA: Walt Disney Productions, 2001. This 1971 movie combines live action and animation. It tells the story of a witch in training and her young friends as they search for a magic spell. The 30th anniversary edition DVD includes restored footage and bonus features.

Harry Potter and the Sorcerer's Stone. Burbank, CA: Warner Home
Video, 2002, DVD. Eleven-year-old Harry Potter leaves behind
an unhappy home life for the Hogwarts School of Witchcraft and
Wizardry. The movie version of J. K. Rowling's first novel uses
some ingenious special effects. But the moody settings, humor, and
strong characters bring the story to life.

The Lord of the Rings: The Motion Picture Trilogy. New York:
New Line Home Video, 2003. New Zealand director Peter
Jackson brings J. R. R. Tolkien's epic battle between good and
evil to the big screen. The boxed DVD set includes extended
editions of *The Fellowship of the Rings, The Two Towers,* and
The Return of the King. Special features include interviews with
cast members, documentaries on costume and art design, behind-
the-scenes photos, and information on Tolkien.

The Wizard of Oz. Burbank, CA: Warner Home Video, 2002,
DVD. This two-disc restored edition of the classic movie contains
several special features. Those include a documentary narrated
by Angela Lansbury, deleted scenes, commentary, trivia, cast
interviews, and a short feature on how the film was restored.

The Witches. Burbank, CA: Warner Home Video, 1999, DVD. Fans
of the book will want to see Roald Dahl's witches in all their
gruesome glory in this 1990 movie. Angelica Huston stars as the
Grand High Witch. Jasen Fisher plays Luke, the boy who tries to
stop the witches with his grandmother, Helga (Mai Zetterling).

Index

About the Author

Ann Kerns has edited many nonfiction books for young readers and is the author of *Australia in Pictures, Romania in Pictures, Martha Stewart,* and *Troy.* She enjoys reading, travel, cooking, and music. A native of Illinois, she is a transplant to Minneapolis, Minnesota.

Photo Acknowledgments